For my kids:
Jill, Brian, Emily, Ashley & Jessie

Special thanks to Jill Malcolm for her technical expertise. I couldn't have done it without you.

gesundheit - [guh-zoo nt-hahyt], interjection, used to wish good health, especially to a person who has just sneezed

The Frog Said Gesundheit

by Lori O'Dea

This is the feather that
tickled Dog's nose,
And made him sneeze
to the tip of his toes,

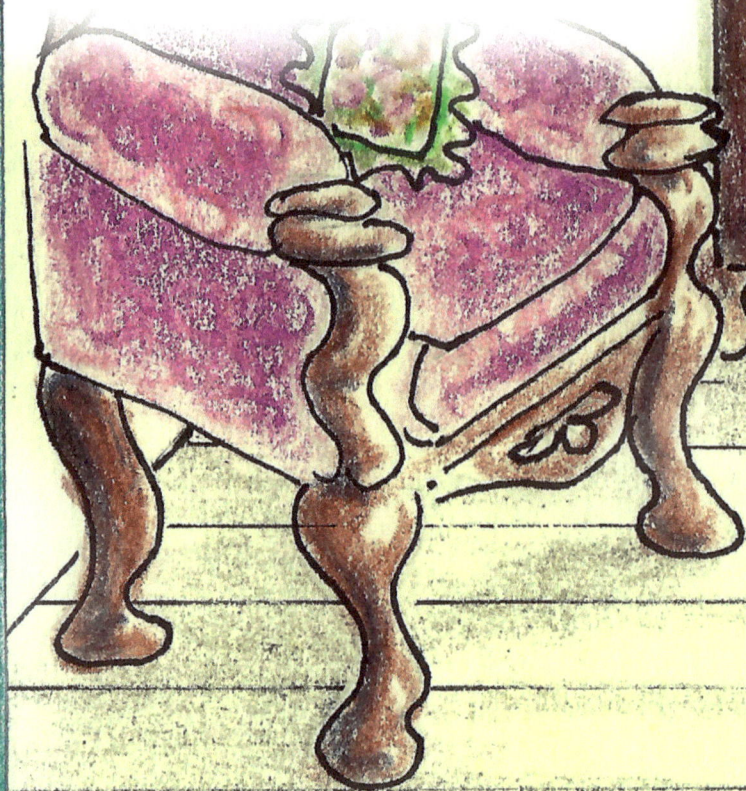

And the frog said,
"Gesundheit!"

This is the goose
that was under the weather
On the fateful day
she lost a feather.
It was this feather that
tickled Dog's nose
And made him sneeze
to the tip of his toes,

And the frog said,
"Gesundheit!"

This is the parrot that got out of his cage,
And squeaked and squawked in such a rage,
He woke poor Goose
    who was under the weather
On the fateful day she lost a feather.
It was this feather that tickled Dog's nose
And made him sneeze to the tip of his toes,

And the frog said,
"Gesundheit!"

This is the hamster that chewed on the cord
It made Parrot's cage fall to the floor,
So he could escape through the open door.
That's how the parrot got out of his cage,
And squeaked and squawked in such a rage,
He woke poor Goose
        who was under the weather,
Causing her sadly to lose a feather.
It was this feather that tickled Dog's nose
And made him sneeze to the tip of his toes,

And the frog said,
"Gesundheit!"

This is the rat that ran from the couch,
Just as Hamster was filling her pouch,
Making her jump, for which I can vouch...
The hamster landed and chewed on the cord
So Parrot escaped when his cage hit the floor.
Squawks woke the goose
      who was under the weather,
Causing poor Goose to lose a feather.
It was this feather that tickled Dog's nose
And made him sneeze to the tip of his toes,

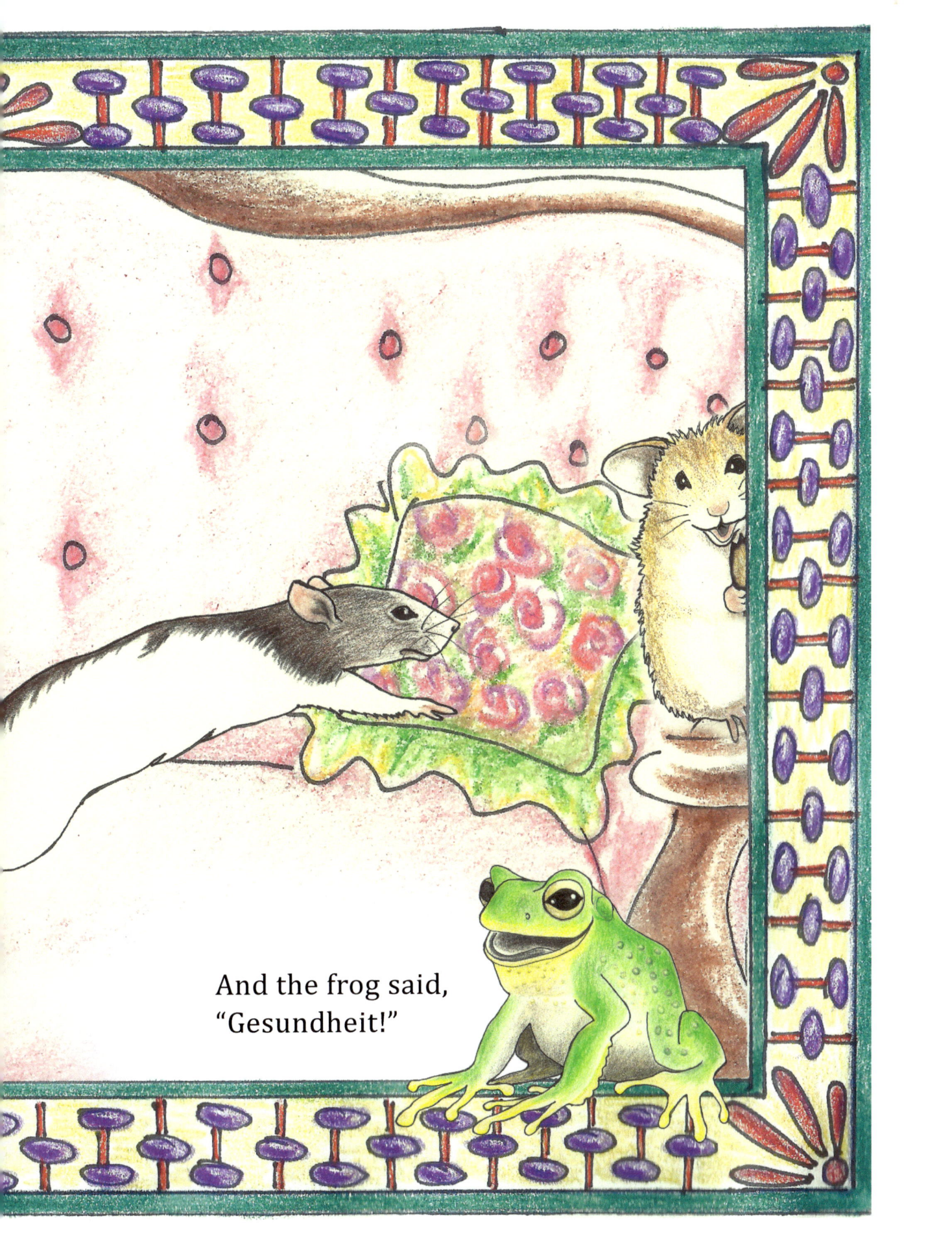

And the frog said,
"Gesundheit!"

This is the cat who lunged at the rat.
He sprang and ran from the couch where he sat,
Just as Hamster was filling her pouch,
Making her jump, for which I can vouch...
She landed and chewed through the cage's cord,
That made Parrot's cage fall to the floor.
Parrot woke Goose
        who was under the weather.
The feverish goose, she lost a feather.
It was this feather that tickled Dog's nose
And made him sneeze to the tip of his toes,

And the frog said,
"Gesundheit!"

This is the lady who screamed so loud,
It scared the cat as she sat so proud.
Without looking up, she lunged at the rat.
The rat, he sprang from the couch where he sat,
Just as Hamster was filling her pouch,
Making her jump, for which I can vouch.
She landed and chewed through the cage's cord,
That made Parrot's cage fall to the floor.
Parrot woke Goose
    who was under the weather,
Causing sick Goose to lose a feather.
It was this feather that tickled Dog's nose
And made him sneeze to the tip of his toes,

And the frog said,
"Gesundheit!"

This is the newt that flew through the air
And landed right in the lady's hair.
It was the lady who screamed so loud,
It scared the cat as she sat so proud.
The cat and rat and hamster too
She jumped to the cage,
        on its cord she did chew.
It made Parrot's cage fall to the floor.
Then noisy Parrot escaped through the door.
Parrot woke Goose who was under the weather,
Causing her sadly to lose a feather.
It was this feather that tickled Dog's nose,
And made him sneeze to the tip of his toes,

And the frog said,
"Gesundheit!"

This is the startled turtle who tramped
Over the base of the table lamp.
The newt was relaxed on the Tiffany shade.
When it toppled over, what a crash it made,
Causing the newt to fly through the air,
And then land right in the lady's hair.
It was the lady who screamed so loud
Which scared the cat, that sat so proud.
The cat, the rat, the hamster nightmare?
The squawking parrot, how did he fare?
He woke the goose that was under the weather.
The shivering goose she lost a feather.
It was this feather that tickled Dog's nose,
And made him sneeze to the tip of his toes,

And the frog said,
"Gesundheit!"

This is the child who let out a whoop,
As something leaped into his bowl of soup.
The trudging turtle was covered with goop...
And that is when the turtle tramped
Over the base of the Tiffany lamp.
The crash sent Newt flying high through the air
And landing right in the lady's hair.
We know the lady then screamed so loud
It scared the cat that sat so proud.
Cat, Rat, Hamster, and Parrot together
Caused the sick goose to lose a feather.
It was this feather that tickled Dog's nose,
And made him sneeze to the tip of his toes,

And the frog said,
"Gesundheit!"

This is the frog who started it all,
When he made a leap from a shelf on the wall.
He landed right in the child's soup,
Which caused the child to let out a whoop.
The turtle, the lamp, the newt flying there
And landing right in the lady's hair.
The lady screamed, she screamed so loud,
The cat and the rat, they both were wowed.
Put Hamster's move and Parrot's together
To cause poor Goose to lose a feather.
It was this feather that tickled Dog's nose,
And made him sneeze to the tip of his toes...

And the frog said...

"Gesundheit!"